Fort Davis and the Texas Frontier

Paintings by Captain Arthur T. Lee, Eighth U.S. Infantry

Entrance to Wild Rose Pass

Fort Davis and the Texas Frontier

Paintings by Captain Arthur T. Lee, Eighth U.S. Infantry

from the collections of THE ROCHESTER HISTORICAL SOCIETY

RUSH RHEES LIBRARY OF THE UNIVERSITY OF ROCHESTER

ROCHESTER MUSEUM AND SCIENCE CENTER

KENNEDY GALLERIES, INC.

Text by W. Stephen Thomas

Published for the AMON CARTER MUSEUM OF WESTERN ART, FORT WORTH

 by the TEXAS A&M UNIVERSITY PRESS, *COLLEGE STATION*

The Amon Carter Museum was established in 1961 under the will of the late Amon G. Carter for the study and documentation of westering North America. The program of the Museum, expressed in publications, exhibitions, and permanent collections, reflects many aspects of American culture, both historic and contemporary.

Library of Congress Cataloging in Publication Data

Lee, Arthur Tracy, d. 1879.
    Fort Davis and the Texas frontier.

    Bibliography: p.
    Includes index.
    1. Lee, Arthur Tracy, d. 1879. 2. Texas in art.
3. Fort Davis, Tex. (Fort) I. Thomas, William Stephen.
II. Title.
ND1839.L38T46   759.13   75-40896
ISBN 0-89096-012-7

Manufactured in the United States of America

FIRST EDITION

Contents

List of Plates

All the works listed, with the exception of the photograph of Lee, two pencil drawings, and one oil painting, as described, are watercolor sketches. Unless otherwise noted, the titles used are those written in pencil, probably by Lee or his descendants, on the sketches themselves or on the mats or scrapbook pages to which the sketches were attached. Titles have been supplied for originally untitled works, and duplicate titles have been numbered.

Preface

Colonel Arthur Tracy Lee (1814–1879) was an experienced and cultured regular Army officer who had extended duty on the southwestern frontier and at the forts and military posts of western Texas before the Civil War. In addition to serving as a regimental officer in the U.S. Eighth Infantry for twenty-three years, twelve of which were spent in Texas, he was a versatile man with sensitive tastes and varied abilities. Artist, author, and musician, his army songs and ballads were sung around campfires from the Seminole and Mexican War days until long after the Civil War. He had the satisfaction of seeing his small book of poetry, *Army Ballads and Other Poems*, printed in 1871, and in the same year his "Reminiscences of the Regiment" appeared in the *History of the Eighth U.S. Infantry*, a literary and handsomely bound book which included that amusing and deftly written account of his life with the Eighth Infantry up to the time of the Civil War. In the late 1860's his appointment as governor of the national Soldiers' Home in the outskirts of Washington, D.C., made him a prominent personality in social and diplomatic circles. Despite these circumstances, which gave him distinction in his own era, the man might have been forgotten today were it not for the vigilance of his family in safely keeping examples of his landscape sketches. Fortunately, his granddaughter and sole surviving relative, Miss Mary Janet Ashley of Rochester, New York, in 1961, five years before her death, gave most of the pictures in this book to three institutions of her home city: the Rochester Historical Society, the Rush Rhees Library of the University of Rochester, and the Rochester Museum and Science Center. Her foresight in preserving these pictorial records makes this book possible.

The bulk of Lee's artistic production consists of 154 sketches on drawing paper averaging five by eight inches in size. Most of the works are in watercolor, with only a few in pencil. Subjects range from landscapes and river scenery to buildings and military outposts in locations such as Mexico, Texas, Wisconsin, Pennsylvania, New York, and Florida. At least 30 of the total are views in Texas. The Rochester Historical society possesses an album of 30 scenes, 21 of which are of Texas and the Rio Grande border and the remainder of the upper Mississippi River country. Mrs. James Sibley Watson, Jr., Director of the Society, has graciously given permission to reproduce them.

The Rush Rhees Library of the University of Rochester, through the courtesy of Ben Bowman, Librarian, and Robert L. Volz, Head of the Department of Rare Books, Manuscripts and Archives, has allowed the use of eighteen Lee pictures from its holdings. Thanks is also due Karl Kabelac, Assistant Librarian in the same department, for his courtesies. The Rochester Museum and Science Center has given permission to reproduce the only known oil painting by Lee, a portrait of Comanche Chief Yellow Wolf, as well as three watercolors. Grateful acknowledgment is made to Richard C. Shultz, Executive Director; Charles F. Hayes III, Director of the Museum; Janice Wass, Associate Librarian; and Stuart Kohler, Assistant Librarian, in making available documents pertaining to Colonel Lee.

Finally, Kennedy Galleries, Inc., New York City, has supplied seven watercolors for use in this collection.

The ultimate concept of a monograph on Lee and the publication of his Texas drawings developed from a letter of Susan Miles, historian of San Angelo, Texas, to the Rochester Museum and Science Center seeking information about Lee. Since then, that lady's kind efforts in suggesting sources of information on Lee's activities in Texas have been most helpful. Barry Scobee, veteran journalist and authority on the early history of Fort Davis, took pains in checking information. Mitchell C. Wilder, Director of the Amon Carter Museum of Western Art in Fort Worth, gave stimulus and encouragement in exhibiting Lee's pictures at his institution. Special thanks go to Ron C. Tyler, Curator of History of that museum, who, over a seven-year period, has proved to be an unfailing source of help and encouragement.

Many scholars and historical experts in Texas have been most cooperative in sharing knowledge. Michael Becker, former Superintendent of the Fort Davis National Historical Site, furnished copies of records of Lee's movements during the period from 1854 to 1858. Of particular importance was the extensive aid of Mildred P. Mayhall of Austin, author of *The Kiowas* and *Indian Wars of Texas*, who copied out lengthy records mentioning Lee's service at Fort Croghan. She also read and criticized the section of this account concerning Lee's relations with the Indians, as did W. W. Newcomb, Director of the Texas Memorial Museum at the University of Texas at Austin.

John C. Ewers, former Director of the U.S. National Museum and ethnologist and authority on the Plains Indians, several times found the answers to difficult questions. Marie T. Capps, Manuscript and Map Librarian of the U.S. Military Academy at West Point, New York, supplied facts on Seth Eastman and other teachers of military drawing.

In Rochester I was most fortunate to have several interviews with Miss Ashley, who recited anecdotes of her grandfather's life. A kind friend who read the manuscript with care and made numerous helpful suggestions was Joseph Barnes, City Historian of Rochester. Others who read the manuscript in the course of its preparation were Dr. and Mrs. James Sibley Watson, Jr., who showed me innumerable kindnesses; Charles F. Hayes III; the late Harris K. Prior, former Director of the Memorial Art Gallery of the University of Rochester; Howard Merritt, former Chairman of the Fine Arts Department of the University of Rochester; and John A. Leermakers, former Vice-President for Research of the Eastman Kodak Company and expert on the history of the Western Plains who put his extensive library at my disposal and helped me in many ways.

Other important sources of help were the directors, librarians, assistant librarians, and curators of museums, libraries, historical societies, and archives in fifteen cities in seven states who were most cooperative in allowing me access to books, newspapers, and documents. One of these was Mrs. H. D. Walter of the Northumberland County Historical Society in Sunbury, Pennsylvania, who supplied information on Colonel Lee's genealogy.

Rochester Museum and Science Center   W.S.T.
January 14, 1975

Fort Davis and the Texas Frontier

Paintings by Captain Arthur T. Lee, Eighth U.S. Infantry

Introduction

THE western frontier of the United States has long been a source of fascination for Americans. A century and more ago it lured them by the thousands. The writer Thoreau once described its attraction in poetic prose that spoke also for many Easterners less articulate than he:

> Every sunset which I witness inspires me with the desire to go to a West as distant and as fair as that into which the sun goes down. He appears to migrate westward daily, and tempt us to follow him. . . . We dream all night of those mountain-ridges in the horizon, though they may be of vapor only, which were last gilded by his rays. The island of Atlantis, and the islands and gardens of the Hesperides, a sort of terrestrial paradise, appear to have been the Great West of the ancients, enveloped in mystery and poetry. Who has not seen in imagination, when looking into the sunset sky, the gardens of the Hesperides, and the foundation of all those fables?[1]

But the western frontier of the United States actually had its inception near the East Coast soon after the founding there of the first settlements. Early pioneers, still seeking fresh opportunity, began venturing farther inland, thus paying no heed to contrary orders from the King of England, who wanted to keep his subjects along a narrow strip of Atlantic Coast where they could be more easily governed from afar.

The movement accelerated as it progressed, and it received addi-

[1] Henry David Thoreau, *The Works of Thoreau*, ed. Henry Seidel Canby (Boston: Houghton Mifflin Co., 1946), p. 669.

tional impetus from some huge land acquisitions: the Northwest Territory, the Louisiana Purchase, Texas, Oregon Territory, and the giant slice of western land acquired from Mexico after the 1846–1848 war. The entire United States seemed to be caught up in chasing Thoreau's poetic sun and, as a coincidental necessity, in eliminating an antagonistic native population of Indians from the path of white immigration.

The westward movement of that rambunctious period long ago settled down to a quiet repose on the silent pages of history books, but its fascination lingers, as is manifested by the countless novels, motion pictures, and television programs that have sought to recreate it—all with varying emphasis on accuracy. Authors of those western stories have found, without looking very hard, many subjects of universal interest: white men contending against an alien, often terrifying land; red men seeking to retain their beloved hunting grounds; and countless glamorous, exciting adventures revealed in the lives of explorers, hunters, miners, immigrants, soldiers, cattlemen, and early farmers who made possible the settling of the American West all the way to the Pacific Coast.

When a sensitive, artistic thirty-four-year-old officer of the United States Army arrived in Texas late in 1848 for what was to be a twelve-year stint, the frontier was real, daily existence was precarious, Indians were a living threat, and western realism, dramatic enough, had not lost much ground to the efforts of diverse fictioneers who have since succeeded in substituting a great deal of legend for fact. Arthur Tracy Lee, an officer attached to the Eighth Infantry Regiment, had received an academic education, probably in his home town of Northumberland, Pennsylvania, and later had studied art. He had received his commission as a second lieutenant in 1838, when he was twenty-four, with the help of an influential member of Congress, Simon Cameron—later Lincoln's Secretary of War. Lee's service before his arrival in Texas included battle action in the Seminole and Mexican wars, but that hard military experience had not made him a "typical" army officer. "He had so many other accomplishments and skills," a newspaper writer said of him, "one could imagine him following any . . . of several professions."[2]

During his military career Lee indeed displayed many other capabilities besides that of soldier. He was also a portrait painter (in oils), watercolorist, poet, musician, essayist, historian, landscape architect, engineer, and administrator. When he came to Texas immediately after the close of the Mexican War he had an opportunity to see and to paint for posterity an area of that western vastness even less familiar than most other new land. His scenes, reproduced here for the first time, depict a region generally ignored, or maybe unseen, by many other artists who were also roaming and sketching the West in those days.

The area Lee thus portrayed was an intriguing one: an arid, isolated, sparsely populated section of Texas west of San Antonio and north of the thirtieth parallel. A few other visitors with artistic bent did record their impressions in paintings and sketches, but they made up a truly small group. Not many travelers chose to stay long in that vicinity, vulnerable as they were to Indian attack and to other dangers.

When Lee arrived in Texas, comparatively few white men had even seen the remote western wilderness he would portray. Texans themselves tended to ignore the area, presuming it to be as worthless as "the Great American Desert" that supposedly covered much of the territory east of the Rockies. Even today that West Texas region shows scant human tampering. It looks much the same as it did then, with the exception of the appearance and growth of scattered towns and cities in a land that proved to be (like "the Great American Desert") not all worthless.

But that country still looks forbidding enough, particularly to a traveler who has come from an area of abundant rainfall. From San Antonio northwestward to El Paso a direct line bisecting it stretches more than five hundred miles. South of that line lies the Big Bend of the Rio Grande; the whole region is a rocky, prickly desert, barren brown during most of the year and cut by only a few reliable streams like the Pecos and the Great River of the North that runs along the Mexican border. In the westernmost part of this country thirsty mountains poke dry, rocky heights above the surrounding wasteland, but in a section north of the Big Bend one range shelters an oasis. The Davis Mountains, lying between the Rio Grande and the Pecos River, cover an area about fifty miles long and forty miles wide, with towering masses of granitic, porphyritic, and volcanic rocks and with limestones of various ages.[3]

But the sharp peaks and abrupt mesas of the Davis Mountains overlook a better country than the arid wilderness that surrounds them. They are wooded on their higher slopes with pine, oak, and cherry and are covered in their lower valleys with spring-and-summer greenery nourished by rainfall sufficient for the purpose—moisture that is remarkable for the trans-Pecos area.[4]

This was the country that Lee saw in its virginity and that he came to love. He helped to establish in those mountains an army post named Fort Davis, maintained for years afterward to guard the safety

[2] Rochester, N.Y., *Union-Advertiser*, December 30, 1879.

[3] Walter Prescott Webb (ed.), *The Handbook of Texas* (Austin: Texas State Historical Association, 1952), I, 472.
[4] Ibid.

4

of travelers seeking the golden promise of Thoreau's western sunset and to contain the local Indian threat as effectively as the minimal numbers of soldiers would allow.

"Beautiful beyond description was the location of Fort Davis . . . and its surroundings," Lee mused years after he had looked upon the scene for the last time:

> A wide deep [canyon], carpeted with the richest verdure, overshadowed by live oak, its lofty and precipitous sides festooned with perennial vines, and mantled with moss and flowers, looking out over smiling prairies and table lands, to miniature lakes, and lofty mountain peaks, that lost their summits in the clouds. Who, with good company, mirth and music, would not have compromised for Fort Davis . . . as a life long resting place? True, it afforded some out door entertainments not always palatable when indulged in to excess; such as early morning drills, over dew mantled grass . . . and fruitless scouts on foot, in pursuit of mounted and swift flying [Indians]. Still, with a fair store of patience . . . they could be endured.
>
> The Limpia valley [nearby] abounded in game, such as deer, snipe, and quail—the latter . . . of beautiful black and mottled plumage, dainty in the choice of its food, much larger than the common quail, and more juicy and delicate. And then the tulegrass lakes of the surrounding prairies, were the summer homes and hatching places of the dainty blue and green winged teal, which afforded abundant sport during the fall, and winter months, to satisfy the most inveterate and insatiable sportsmen. . . .[5]

During his tour of duty Lee sketched his impressions of this isolated region in a series of charming watercolors that depicted the far-away country few people had even seen. In his pictures Lee gave the western country an arid vastness that can be felt as well as seen. Sun-bleached landscapes, seeming to shimmer in the day's heat, dwarf detailed figures of men and animals. A comparison of his West Texas scenes with those from other localities will show the effect Lee obviously sought to give.

The versatile man who painted these pictures remains almost unknown. During his lifetime he was a personage, to a degree, not only in the army but in some circles outside it, yet today no diaries or personal letters written by him are known to exist. He is not included in any biographical dictionaries. His name does not appear in accounts written by army superiors, some of whom he knew personally.

A few of Lee's characteristics may be deduced after an examination of the scant information available about him. A rare photograph, obviously made in.later years, shows an aging, oval-faced man with wavy hair, ample beard and moustache, and time-bleached, liquid eyes that seem to indicate sensitivity and sympathy—qualities that are also reflected in his writing as preserved in two published works: *Army Ballads and Other Poems*, and "Reminiscences of the Regiment," in *History of the Eighth U.S. Infantry*, both published in 1871.

One may draw conclusions in a similar way about a few other traits. Lee was a spirited man with firm convictions, as was proved twice during his tour of duty in Texas when he was placed under military arrest apparently because of disagreement with his commanding officer—once for a period of three months and again for several days.

His painting and writing also attest to his spirit. Lee's prose contains hints of an obvious talent for making friends and for winning popularity. His nature would have been lively and responsive, certainly so because we know that he liked to join in on a song and that he played the violin. His intellectual interests and artistic skills would have given him many outlets for enrichment and enjoyment and would have made much more endurable some of the waiting required of the career military man. But family tragedies certainly saddened him from time to time and would have dampened his enthusiasm, if only temporarily. He and his wife, who accompanied him to

---

[5] Arthur T. Lee, "Reminiscences of the Regiment," in *History of the Eighth U.S. Infantry*, ed. Thomas Wilhelm (New York, 1871), II, 365–367.

the rugged Texas frontier, lost three of their young children during his army career.

Slow promotion must have proved frustrating. Lee was seven years a second lieutenant and thirteen years a captain. His promotion during the Civil War was so slow that a home-town journalist wrote, ". . . [Lee] has probably performed as much labor as any man in the service. . . . With all this, he only reached the position of major. . . . Meanwhile, officers who have not done half so much or as well have gone from lieutenant to major-general. . . ."[6]

Still, Lee enjoyed a colorful army career. Early in his service, in 1839, he had duty on the Saint Lawrence River during the "Patriot War," a flare-up against Britain that attracted the support along the Canadian border of many Americans always eager to fight their old enemy. In the spring and summer of the next year Lee accompanied his regiment to Wisconsin to assist in the removal of the unwanted Winnebago Indians. During the next three years he helped in hunting bands of Seminole Indians in Florida swamps while at the same time writing melancholic ballads on the sad fate of those very people who were suffering at the hands of Lee and his white colleagues. From September, 1845, to April, 1846, Lee was in Texas with the "army of occupation" sent by the United States to ensure the safety and security of the former republic about to be annexed to the North American union despite war threats from Mexico. During the conflict that did indeed follow, he commanded a company of the Eighth Infantry in the battles of Palo Alto and Resaca de la Palma and was brevetted to the rank of captain upon recommendation by General Zachary Taylor. From September, 1846, to July, 1848, Lee was assigned as a recruiting officer in the northeastern United States; in late summer and fall of 1848 he was given detached duty in connection with the second removal of Winnebago Indians, this time from Minnesota. Then came Lee's long period of service on the Texas frontier

[6] Rochester, N.Y., *Union and Advertiser*, August 10, 1866.

that brought him a variety of duties as post commander and deputy commander and builder of forts and sent him on Indian scouting and punitive expeditions over a wide range of territory.

During the Civil War Lee was captured and held by Confederates for a time before being paroled. After his return to the North, his wartime assignments ranged from mustering and disbursing duty to drilling recruits and, after his release from parole, to commanding troops in the battle at Gettysburg, where he was severely wounded. From 1867 until 1872 he was assigned as administrator of the Soldiers' Home in Washington.

Lee lived seven years longer. He and his wife resided near a daughter, Katherine, and her husband, William J. Ashley, in Rochester, New York. But during summer seasons Lee boarded at Shelter Island, New York, at the eastern end of Long Island. There he devoted much time to painting—making watercolor sketches of the eastern landscape and copies of the western scenes he remembered vividly from his army days on the frontier that had attracted him and so many other Americans and that continues to fascinate a large part of the population today.

Soldiering in Texas

Among the many reasons for the growth of the West Texas frontier was a burgeoning trade with Mexico. In the first half of the nineteenth century, commercialism flourishing in the city of Santa Fe and in other areas of the then-Spanish Southwest attracted adventurous and daring men from the Missouri frontier and from other places farther east. These men—scouts, explorers, traders—followed the long trail leading into Mexico, using a route across the arid southwestern region that enabled them to avoid the dreaded Staked Plain, a sea of grass empty of shelter, wood, and water.

Long before the appearance of white men, however, this area was familiar ground to Comanche Indians, whose warpaths for invading present-day Mexico extended from the Comanche range near the headwaters of the Arkansas and Red rivers into Mexico as far as Durango. The Great Comanche War Trail is significant in West Texas history, for it had made the Indians thoroughly familiar with the region and it accounted for the vulnerability of several routes leading west across Texas.

After the Mexican War had ended and a vast western territory had been acquired by the United States, it became necessary to find new routes to California. Discovery of gold there in 1848 coincided with the end of Mexican hostilities, and large numbers of emigrants headed for the Pacific Coast. Many chose routes that took them through Texas, but in their travels across the westernmost part of the state they took many risks. Enormous distances had to be covered. Water was scarce; so was forage for oxen, mules, and horses. Hostile Indians threatened constantly. Nevertheless, people by the thousands were using that southern route in 1849. One observer said, "By July [1849] there was an immense concourse of emigrants at El Paso, upwards of four thousand, with from twelve to fifteen hundred wagons all camped up and down the river at one time."[7]

The flood of emigration forced the United States government to initiate two important measures: establishment of a road leading from San Antonio through mountainous West Texas, and assignment of the army to the task of protecting lives and property of settlers on the Texas frontier from marauding Comanches, Kiowas, and Apaches. The army began extending its line of forts and outposts although it was operating under a great manpower handicap. At the end of the Mexican War its numbers had been reduced from 30,890 to 10,320, and a decade later, even after some augmentation, only one soldier was available to guard every 120 square miles of western land.[8]

On December 5, 1848, Fort Martin Scott was established two miles south of the German settlement of Fredericksburg, Texas, on Baron's Creek, a confluent of the Pedernales River. Its purpose was to protect the Fredericksburg–San Antonio Road. Next the army established Fort Duncan just above Eagle Pass. Northeastward from there soldiers also manned a ring of forts located outside several settlements, including Fort Inge, near the present town of Uvalde;

---

[7] J. Evetts Haley, *Fort Concho and the Texas Frontier* (San Angelo, Texas: San Angelo *Standard-Times*, 1952), p. 51.

[8] Leonard Wood, *Our Military History: Its Facts and Fallacies* (Chicago: Reilly and Britton, 1916), pp. 147, 149.

Fort Croghan, near present Burnet; Fort Gates, about five miles east of present Gatesville; Fort Graham, on the Brazos River about fourteen miles west of present Hillsboro; and Fort Worth (named for William Jenkins Worth, the commander of Captain Arthur T. Lee's Eighth Regiment).[9] These forts constituted a line of defense that presumably guaranteed the safety of Texas settlers, but scattered groups of Indians, mostly Comanches, Kiowas, and Apaches, constantly broke through to strike quick blows. After raiding, they usually fled at once for the safety of their plains homes.

Despite the dangers, emigrants had worn a trail between San Antonio and El Paso by 1849. Further, the War Department had conducted some preliminary surveys in the area for a transcontinental railway. All this activity encouraged settlement in western Texas, but it also alarmed the Indians and caused them to increase their hostilities. Military force in the area soon proved to be much too thin to police the Indians. More soldiers came.

For this reason the newly arrived Eighth Regiment of U.S. Infantry, including Captain Lee, found itself encamped for three months early in 1849 at a post called Worth (but not Fort Worth) located on the San Antonio River. The army had begun setting up new posts and moving forward its supply depots over a large area.

At the same time, however, the existing line of fortifications had to be maintained. A West Texas historian described the situation:

> . . . the troops in Texas were more like an army in the field in active war than in garrison. The regular force had been increased by an auxiliary, volunteer force and had been furnished with supplies, with extensive means of transportation . . . and with horses to mount a portion of the foot soldiers. But, the territory of the Big Bend was so vast, the troops employed for its defense, as well as the defense of the [wagon] trains which supplied the various posts on the frontier, had to traverse routes so long and so unimproved that the expense of transportation and all supplies was extremely heavy. . . .[10]

Captain Lee also wrote a description of army activity during this period, one saddened for him by the sudden death, on May 7, 1849, of his regimental commander, William J. Worth: "A few fleeting months, and the white tents of Camp Worth were no longer reflected in the clear waters of the San Antonio. Scattered to the winds, they bleached and browned in the sun and rains of Camp Lincoln, on the Rio Frio, Fort Inge, on the Las Moras, Fort Croghan, . . . near the Colorado, Fort Gates, near the Cowhouse, and Fort Graham, on the Rio Brazos. These posts, with Fort Martin Scott, comprised at that time all the out-posts of Texas."[11]

After the brief encampment at the post called Worth, and until the Eighth Regiment was ordered westward to the Limpia River in 1854, Captain Lee and soldiers of his C Company were stationed at six different frontier locations. During much of that time Lee was also on detached service—on court-martial duty in Austin in late July and early August, 1851, and in the East on extensive leave with his family from January to October, 1853.

Detailed examination of Lee's activities during the five-year period shows that he seems to have been at Fort Croghan from October, 1849, through most of 1850. This post was located on Hamilton Creek, a tributary of the Colorado. Although official army records state that the fort was established on March 18, 1849, by Brevet Second Lieutenant Charles H. Tyler of the Second Dragoons, Lee's military record shows that he "built" the fort in the fall of 1849.[12] This

[9] Haley, *Fort Concho*, p. 51.

[10] Carlysle Graham Raht, *The Romance of Davis Mountains and Big Bend Country* (Odessa, Texas: Rahtbooks, 1963), p. 93.

[11] Lee, "Reminiscences," II, 344.

[12] Robert W. Frazer, *Forts of the West* (Norman: University of Oklahoma Press, 1965), p. 148.

apparent inconsistency may be due to the possibility that the post originally consisted of tents or huts, as was often the case, and that Lee supervised the construction of permanent buildings.

The official regimental history lists Captain Lee as "commanding" at Fort Croghan on January 31, 1851,[13] but during most of February and the last part of March, 1851, he was at Fort Martin Scott. For a brief period that spring, from February 29 to March 13, Lee was on detached service at Fort Graham, but he returned to Fort Martin Scott and with C and E companies left on May 20, 1851, to arrive at Fort Croghan three days later. From July 29 to August 7 he was assigned to court-martial duty in Austin. He must have returned to Fort Croghan in late summer—and evidently his family had been there for some time. His only child to survive into adult life, Katherine Whitney Lee (later known as Kate), was born at a house near the fort on November 29, 1851.[14]

On February 15, 1852, Lee's infantrymen and four other companies of the Eighth Regiment, all under command of Major Pitcairn M. Morrison, left Fort Croghan for Fort Mason, where they arrived on February 19. Fort Mason was located two miles west of Comanche Creek and eight miles above its confluence with the Llano River. After a two-week stay there the five companies left Mason on March 6, 1852, bound for a post to be established on the North Concho River—Camp Johnston. Thereafter, any monotony of spring and summer camp life would have been relieved by friendly, official visits with a large group of Southern Comanche Indians known as "Honey Eaters." But Lee later remembered also a few unpleasant aspects of his sojourn on the Concho:

> Snakes, tornadoes, air quakes, hail storms, shotted with boulders like goose eggs, floods, stampedes, and Indian pow-wows, were the

excitements of Camp Johnstone [sic], until the late fall of [1852], when General Persifor Smith, then commanding the Department of Texas, convinced himself by a personal visit, of a fact, which no previous correspondence could induce him to believe, or at least acknowledge, that there were no forests . . . within, forty miles of the Concho, nor any kind of material for building purposes, and ordered its abandonment to the joy of all concerned, for a location forty miles north, on Oak Creek—so named from a sparse covering of scrub post-oak, and black-jack, which infested and disfigured its banks; but afforded material, such as it was, sufficient for the construction of a military post, afterwards known as Fort Chadbourne.[15]

Only one or two companies were with Lee when he arrived at the site of Chadbourne in the late fall of 1852. His military record states that he established the fort in December, 1852,[16] although a recent author says that Fort Chadbourne was established on October 28, 1852.[17] Chadbourne was situated on the east side of Oak Creek about three miles above its junction with the Colorado River and approximately four miles northeast of the present town of Fort Chadbourne. By January 10, Eighth Infantry headquarters had been officially located at that place and remained there until summer.

Lee returned from an 1853 leave of absence in the East to a new station. Regimental headquarters, the band, and four companies were moved from Fort Chadbourne four hundred miles southward to Ringgold Barracks, near Rio Grande City. One pictorial record of Lee's stay there is a watercolor sketch of the nearby town (Plate 6). The drawing seemingly depicts a small, peaceful settlement, but the artist-soldier wrote that Rio Grande City "could boast more crimes of murder, robbery, assassination, and outlawry generally, than all the rest of the Texan cities . . . including Corpus Christi."[18]

---

[13] Thomas Wilhelm, *Synopsis of the History of the Eighth U.S. Infantry and the Military Record of Officers* (David's Island, N.Y., 1871), p. 41.

[14] Francis Bacon Trowbridge, *The Ashley Genealogy* (New Haven, 1896), p. 280.

[15] Lee, "Reminiscences," II, 354–355.

[16] Wilhelm, *Synopsis of the History of the Eighth U.S. Infantry*, p. 280.

[17] Frazer, *Forts of the West*, p. 145.

[18] Lee, "Reminiscences," II, 356–357.

Years later, when recalling an incident of his stay at Ringgold, Lee showed a faculty for describing scenes in nature almost as well with the pen as with the brush:

> Whilst the abundant and beautiful, but unpalatable fruit of the pricklypear, was crimsoning in the sun of August '53; when the purple breasted wood pigeon unfolded its wings to the hot breath of the lazy breeze, as it came loitering over the prairies, and clung panting on the limb of the thorny mesquite, and the swallow dipped in vain its hot beak for a cooling sip in the shallow waters of the Rio Grande . . . came orders from Department Headquarters, directing an immediate movement of the companies of the Eighth at Ringgold, up the river to occupy certain Indian crossings, somewhere between Roma and Eagle Pass. . . .[19]

Little information is available about the Eighth Regiment during its stay of some ten months on the Rio Grande. Part of that time Captain Lee was in temporary command. Although no detailed accounts of his adventures during this period exist, there survive two sketches probably done at the time on trips to the upper waters of the Rio Grande (Plates 7, 8).

In the summer of 1854, apparently, word came that an important movement of troops would be made because of the need to establish a permanent fort high in the mountain fastnesses to the west in what were then called the Apache Mountains, now the Davis Mountains. A small force under Brevet Major General Persifor F. Smith would move out to look over an area of West Texas. A larger force, which was to include Captain Lee, would meet Smith at a designated location in the mountains. The six-hundred-mile march of Lee's group, made up of six companies of mounted riflemen under the overall command of Lieutenant Colonel Washington Seawell, required six weeks.[20]

[19] Ibid., pp. 361–362.

[20] Raht, *Romance of Davis Mountains*, p. 134.

Into the Mountains

CAPTAIN LEE's first view of the Davis Mountains left a lifetime impression. Land masses of the Davis Range rise in "irregular order, mountain on mountain, and peak on peak, covering an immense extent of country, and forming innumerable, small and shaded valleys, deep canyons, and ravines."[21] The mountains rise to heights of three thousand feet above the surrounding plateau.[22]

Traveling up a canyon named Limpia to the vicinity of Wild Rose Pass on October 3, 1854, Lee saw awesome walls of volcanic rock towering a thousand feet and more above him. But he and the other members of Lieutenant Colonel Seawell's force quickly became aware of a danger in that awesome scenery. Mescalero Apaches had hidden themselves on those heights and now opened fire with arrows that were given sufficient force to tear through a man's body. The Indians, alarmed by the appearance of increasing numbers of emigrants and their long wagon trains, by stagecoaches and drivers, and by soldiers, had determined to defend their country. They used the heights of Limpia Canyon, through which travelers in the area had to pass, for their ambushes. No white man's life had been safe there for months, and repeated requests had been sent to Washington for establishment of an army post at this location to protect mail carriers and travelers.[23] Now the soldiers sent for that very purpose were forced to fight their way through the canyon, too.

They took cover and fought back. Their superior weapons won them a passage, but for a time it was a bitterly disputed one. Finally they joined General Smith and his escort and "spread out [a white camp] on the green valley that nestled under the frown of the black Sierra."[24] Their situation was high and remote; they were at an elevation of 4,900 feet with mountains surrounding them, 475 miles from San Antonio to the southeast and 220 miles from El Paso to the northwest—their nearest supply bases.

Four days after their arrival Fort Davis was officially established and named. The first buildings were located in a picturesque setting under Crouching Lion Mountain, beneath a mountainside of "rust colored . . . igneous rock with its rugged, palisaded front" that made a natural amphitheater in which the fort buildings were set.[25]

The site had been decided upon by General Smith while he awaited Seawell's force. On October 23, 1854, the general issued Special Order No. 129, Department of Texas, establishing Fort Davis. The order was dated at Painted Camp, a location one mile northeast of the fort on the Limpia River. The camp name came from Apache and Comanche Indian paintings on the trunks of large cottonwoods nearby; the fort was named for Jefferson Davis, then secretary of war.[26]

Availability of other trees for use in construction was a first con-

[21] Raht, *Romance of Davis Mountains*, p. 88.
[22] William Trout Chambers, *The Geography of Texas* (Austin: Steck Co., 1946), p. 198.
[23] Barry Scobee, *Old Fort Davis* (San Antonio: The Naylor Co., 1947), p. 8.

[24] Lee, "Reminiscences," II, 364.
[25] R. P. Conkling and M. B. Conkling, *The Butterfield Overland Mail, 1857–1869* (Glendale, Calif.: Arthur H. Clark Co., 1947), II, 27.
[26] Scobee, *Old Fort Davis*, p. 4.

sideration. On surrounding mountains oak and pine thrived, but the only trees in the vicinity of the fort site were some cottonwoods. In an effort to obtain enough wood to build log huts and houses for officers and men, Lieutenant Richard Irving Dodge and a detail of men scoured hills nearby for timber suitable for "saw-logs."[27] Other details of men ventured farther out, and they found a suitable stand of timber twenty-five miles away. Logs were cut there and then brought in mule-drawn wagons to the vicinity of the fort to a Page circular sawmill powered by twelve more mules, where they were cut into slabs.[28]

All these woodsmen must have scoured efficiently, because three years later Lieutenant Thomas Marshall Jones, writing about Fort Davis, mentioned a lawsuit brought by the owner of that forested land, one John James, against Jones, Lee, and another officer to compensate for the value of those logs cut by soldiers. In time the government paid.[29]

Even before this temporary construction commenced, Colonel Seawell had questioned the wisdom of the fort's location—in a narrow, high-walled canyon that left it open to Indian attack—and he continued to protest the selection. Seawell hoped to move Fort Davis to a safer site, but a year and a half later, in August, 1856, Captain Lee, who had been left in temporary command while Seawell was away, gave orders to begin construction of six barracks of fieldstone. Right or wrong, this action finally determined the permanent location. It might also have accounted for one of Lee's two arrests. Lee admitted that he did not get along well with this superior officer.[30]

Despite the vulnerability and isolation of the site, Fort Davis's location gave it some advantages: good climate, well-nourished vegetation, and picturesqueness from the sheer cliffs and mountain peaks looming nearby. Two scenic spots near Fort Davis made such an impression on Lee that he not only mentioned them in his writing but also sketched them several times. One was a peak Lee called Sierra Prieta, or Black Mountain, the tallest in the vicinity, flanking the entrance to Wild Rose Pass. Lee described it as "long looked for" on the six-week march from the Rio Grande and called it "the mammoth of the Limpia Hills."[31] One of his sketches shows the mountain with an Indian encampment in the foreground (Plate 9). The other shows a group of mules and oxen grazing in the foreground and Fort Davis lying in the distance (Plate 11).

The other scenic area that intrigued Lee was Wild Rose Pass, described by him as "a gorgeous hall of lofty palisades, ten miles in length, and looking down upon [Fort Davis]."[32] Of this area he made two sketches. One shows the canyon trail leading into Wild Rose Pass and, on the trail, five covered wagons drawn by mule teams (frontispiece). The other sketch focuses on the trees growing in the pass (Plate 10).

Since Lee had an inquiring mind, he may have known the recent history of the pass and how it was named on March 19, 1849, by William H. C. Whiting, a lieutenant of engineers. Whiting and another lieutenant, Francis T. Bryan, a small party of frontiersmen, and two interpreters had been detailed to find a suitably watered emigrant route through West Texas for people on their way to California. In early darkness the party entered a defile of the Davis Mountains. Whiting wrote of what they saw the next morning: "The daylight showed us on awaking a fine pass. . . . wild roses, the only ones I had seen in Texas, grew luxuriantly. I named the defile, 'Wild Rose Pass,' and the brook, the 'Limpia.' We followed it through the range,

[27] Richard Irving Dodge, *Our Wild Indians: Thirty-three Years' Personal Experience among the Red Men of the Great West* (Hartford, Conn.: A. D. Worthington, 1882).

[28] Robert M. Utley, *Fort Davis National Historic Site, Texas* (Washington, D.C.: Department of the Interior, National Park Service, 1965), p. 7.

[29] Scobee, *Old Fort Davis*, p. 20.

[30] Ibid., pp. 8, 15.

[31] Lee, "Reminiscences," II, 364.

[32] Ibid.

delighted at the promise of a successful passage where wood and water should obtain in plenty. . . ."[33]

Pleasant also was the Fort Davis climate. It could be cold in winter because of the elevation, but snow was usually no great problem. Altogether, it was a most agreeable place, as Lee had realized at once, and it attracted his artist's eye. Of the thirty or more extant watercolors he painted of Texas scenery, at least sixteen were of Fort Davis or views in the near vicinity. During his entire tour of duty at Fort Davis —from October, 1854, until September, 1858 (with occasional absences for temporary assignment elsewhere)—the countryside fascinated him. As an additional benefit he had the company of his family during most of that time. It was no wonder, then, that for Lee, at least, life at Fort Davis proved more satisfying than at any other post he had been assigned to. As he said, he found available there "good company, mirth and music."[34]

[33] William H. C. Whiting, "Journal of William Henry Chase Whiting, 1849," in *Exploring Southwestern Trails, 1846–1854*, ed. Ralph P. Bieber (Glendale, Calif.: Arthur H. Clark Co., 1938), p. 279.

[34] Lee, "Reminiscences," II, 366.

Life at Fort Davis

WHEN established, Fort Davis was an encampment instead of a fort. Men spent the first winter in tents; nothing sturdier had been completed. The first post was not built where most of the ruins lie today (known now as the Fort Davis National Historic Site), but in a location called Hospital Canyon which lies just west of, and behind, the present line of officers' residences. An old document describes the canyon as "about 3-4s mile long and 400 yrds. wide at its mouth, gradually narrowing to its termination in a recess of the mountains . . . which . . . on either side are formed of metamorphic rocks about 250 ft. high, very rough and precipitous and covered with grass and small oak trees . . . while . . . the surrounding country is wild and barren, without trees . . . except a few cottonwoods on the Limpia."[35]

The first permanent buildings, when finally completed, were said to have been built of rough, dark stone and given thatched roofing.[36] As Lieutenant Richard Irving Dodge had noted, soldiers also erected log structures. Second Lieutenant (later General) Zenas Randall Bliss, a native of Rhode Island stationed at Fort Davis from 1855 to 1861, described in his memoirs the log huts that served as living quarters for younger officers of the garrison when he arrived. They were austere shelters fifteen feet square and six feet high. Cracks caused by warped and shrunken wood allowed the often wild West Texas wind to blow through the interiors. Panes of white cotton cloth, not glass, went into the windows.

In April of the following year, 1856, Colonel Joseph K. F. Mansfield, inspector general of the army, visited the fort and reported that soldiers were still living in wooden huts (*jacales*) and tents eighteen months after the Eighth Regiment had established the post. But Mansfield also mentioned the six new barracks built under Captain Lee's direction; they measured 30 × 60 feet and had stone floors and grass-thatched roofs. In the rear of each building was a slab shack, 30 × 56 feet, that served as kitchen and mess hall.[37] One of Lee's sketches shows a few buildings that look something like this description (Plate 19).

What quarters Lee occupied at the fort is a question that cannot be answered now, but it is known that by July 16, 1857, when he returned to Davis after a leave of absence of sixty days, he had his family with him. The Lees probably lived in a residence somewhat similar to that occupied by the post commander, Colonel Seawell, since Lee was second in command and for the period from August 30, 1856, to March 31, 1857, had served as acting commander. Seawell lived in a comparatively spacious house with board floors, which would have been considered a luxury, indeed. By 1857 other buildings had been constructed at the fort, too, including storehouses, stables, corrals, and a twenty-by-eighty-five-foot hospital made of pickets and thatched with grass.

Because of the remote location of Fort Davis, good food was not

[35] Scobee, *Old Fort Davis*, p. 12.
[36] Conkling and Conkling, *Butterfield Overland Mail*, II, 188.

[37] J. K. F. Mansfield, "Colonel J. K. F. Mansfield's Report on the Inspection of the Department of Texas in 1856," ed. M. L. Crimmins, *Southwestern Historical Quarterly* 42 (April, 1939): 351–357.

easily obtained in the early days. Beef seems to have been the main food item most of the time; the soldiers ate five thousand pounds of it each month at a contracted price of fifteen cents a pound. Beans costing $2.48 a bushel and flour selling for twelve and one-half cents a pound came from Mexico.[38] Lieutenant Bliss described other main fare: salt pork, peas, rice, sugar, and coffee.[39] Bliss also mentioned the availability of watermelons,[40] and Colonel Mansfield spoke of a post garden. Further, officers—and no doubt enlisted men, too—supplemented the simple daily menu with game: deer, antelope, quail, doves, and ducks. Fresh fish for post tables came from the Limpia River and small ponds nearby.

As always, however, officers and their families lived better, generally, than did enlisted men. Occupying a private residence was a comparative luxury, but a major problem emanated from this privilege. Good civilian servant help was almost impossible to find at Fort Davis, and officers' families were forced to rely on the part-time employment of soldiers seeking to earn pocket money. Occasionally in antebellum days officers, including Northerners, owned slaves to perform duties as domestics. Captain Lee was one such owner, although possibly not while he was stationed at Fort Davis. There exists a deed of a gift of slaves from Lee to his wife: a twenty-four year-old woman named Harriet and three children aged six, four, and seventeen months. The deed was dated August 22, 1859, at San Antonio,[41] where Lee was on leave from Fort Quitman after leaving Davis.

More specific information about living conditions at Fort Davis came from Lieutenant Bliss in his memoirs. Life there, he said, "was very different from anything I had experienced at other posts." A shortage of female companionship certainly would have made his stay there more severe. He mentioned the presence of only three women, including Mrs. Arthur T. Lee, and all of them were married. Equally scarce, he said, were parties or other entertainment, although he added that in 1856 soldiers built a post theater that seated about two hundred persons for performances in which members of the garrison did all the acting. Bliss also wrote of a track for "scrub races."[42]

Some early diversion at Fort Davis stemmed from the presence of Albert J. Myer, an army surgeon who had worked as a telegraph operator before entering military (and medical) service and who still maintained an interest in communications. Four months after establishment of the fort, he arrived for duty, observed the surrounding heights, and took advantage of the terrain to begin experimenting with long-distance visual signaling. His work later led to the establishment of the Army Signal Corps, and he became its first chief signal officer.[43]

Other description of Davis and some adjacent forts came from the wife of a Lieutenant Lane of a rifle regiment. She visited Fort Davis on August 12, 1858, while on her way west from Fort Clark to Santa Fe, New Mexico, and she remarked that the officers' wives she met at Fort Davis and other posts along her route seemed contented and comfortable. But she added an observation that although surroundings were beautiful, quarters were very bad. Nevertheless, "kindness and hospitality" abounded at all these places, and travelers like her usually received presents of butter, eggs, and milk.[44]

[38] Utley, *Fort Davis*, p. 9.

[39] Henry I. Kurtz, "A Soldier's Life," *American History*, August, 1972, p. 27.

[40] Zenas Randall Bliss, "Reminiscences of Zenas R. Bliss, Major General United States Army," typescript copy in University of Texas Library Archives, Austin.

[41] Deed in the library of the Rochester, N.Y., Museum and Science Center.

[42] Bliss, "Reminiscences of Zenas R. Bliss."

[43] James M. Day, "Fort Davis," in *Frontier Forts of Texas* (Waco: Texian Press, 1966), p. 120.

[44] Lydia Spencer Lane, *I Married a Soldier* (Albuquerque, N.M.: Wallace Publications, 1964), p. 44.

Still other description of Fort Davis came from Lee himself in "Reminiscences of the Regiment," although that piece of writing contains surprisingly few specifics regarding his days at the fort he helped to establish. He wrote: "[Fort Davis] afforded some out door entertainments not always paiatable when indulged in to excess; such as early morning drills, over dew mantled grass, not deemed essential by captains and subalterns, and fruitless scouts on foot, in pursuit of mounted and swift flying arabs of the prairie wilds. Still, with a fair store of patience, and liberal consideration for old [fogyism], they could be endured."[45]

Officers and enlisted men performed the usual garrison chores: guard duty, caring for army animals, drilling, and scouting, which meant sending out small parties to patrol trails against Indian attack or to pursue and punish Indians when they raided overland caravans or the mail. For performing garrison duties enlisted men received from nine to twelve dollars a month and labored most of the time from sunrise to 8:30 P.M. taps.[46]

A major task was supplying aid and comfort to the emigrant caravans forever chasing Thoreau's setting sun. This job consisted specifically of providing food for animals and people on the move and of making repairs on wagons and other equipment. Ruined harnesses were mended, broken wheels—and entire wagons—were fixed. Inspector General Mansfield noted in April, 1856, that since the founding of the fort not even two years earlier approximately $42,000 in government money had gone to feed impoverished travelers and to renew their outfits—this in a day when a dollar included one hundred valuable pennies. To enable Fort Davis personnel to fulfill their duties toward these emigrants, the army kept a large amount of stock there: "172 mules, 4 horses, 1 ass and 10 captured Indian ponies," and to look after these animals there were "one civilian blacksmith,

a guide, two clerks, two hostlers, three herders, two teamsters and one saddler."[47]

Constant demand and danger came from Indian fighting, usually in the mountains against small bands of Apaches who liked to dismount for the skirmish. But though the risk was continually present, the number of actual encounters was not as great as one might have expected. Lee himself apparently never engaged in combat with Indians while stationed at Fort Davis—at least no records extant show it—but the captain would have been constantly concerned about the possibility and he certainly would have kept himself informed of scouting activity. One noteworthy incident that occurred near the fort in the fall of 1854 was described by Lieutenant Richard Irving Dodge. A reconnaissance party of three privates, one sergeant, and a civilian scout named Sam Cherry went out to look over the countryside. A twelve-year-old boy accompanied them, apparently out of curiosity.

The group failed to return. Later, all their bodies were found riddled with bullets and badly mutilated. Signs showed that they had been attacked by a party of some thirty mounted Indians. The boy apparently had done something to incite the Indians' wrath. Before he died he had been tortured—probably by women, who were adept at the practice. They had forced pine knots into his skin and had set them afire. The boy's body was found tied to a tree, where he had been left to endure his agonizing death.[48]

Although Lee took part in little or no Indian fighting, his life at Fort Davis was not without turmoil, which centered around an apparent clash of personalities and attitudes between Lee and his commanding officer, Lieutenant Colonel Seawell, a graduate of the military academy. Lee's construction of stone barracks at the location opposed by Seawell hinted at the conflict.

[45] Lee, "Reminiscences," II, 366.
[46] Utley, *Fort Davis*, p. 27.

[47] Mansfield, "Colonel J. K. F. Mansfield's Report," p. 355.
[48] Dodge, *Our Wild Indians*, pp. 524–525.

Fort Davis post returns of 1854–1861 in the National Archives indicate at least an extreme disagreement between Seawell and Lee. From December, 1854, until March, 1855—even before Lee ordered construction of those barracks—Lee was placed under arrest for some reason not given in the returns. Soon afterward, the same documents show, Lee was given a sixty-day leave, no doubt by the same Seawell, who would have been glad to see the captain go. The leave lasted from July to September, 1855.

After Lee ordered construction of the barracks in 1856 he found himself in trouble again. Seawell returned to Fort Davis on March 31, 1857, resumed command, and one week later, on April 7, placed Lee under arrest again. Five days later the arrest was suspended, but, significantly, Lee left on another sixty-day leave on April 20.

Still, Captain Lee's duty at Fort Davis was more pleasant than disagreeable, as he indicated in his "Reminiscences." During the three years and eleven months of his residence there he had a total time away on leave (for whatever reason) of six months. Usually his family accompanied him on these vacations. Some of this time was spent in San Antonio, where diversions were comparatively plentiful. Always, however, Lee seemed ready to return to Fort Davis and to its relative austerity: occasional horse races and amateur theatricals, infrequent concerts given by a thirteen-man military band, and two mail deliveries a week—once each from the east and from the west.

The mail came by coach, which usually carried passengers, too. These visitors eagerly mingled with fort personnel and passed on the latest information from other parts of the country. Their arrivals and the comings and goings of emigrants afforded the garrison entertainment, excitement, and even enlightenment. But the most unusual arrival at Fort Davis during Lee's stay there was a herd of humpbacked animals.

The Camel Experiment

IN July of 1857 a caravan of twenty-five camels arrived at Fort Davis bound from an army post near San Antonio for California. The animals were accompanied by a strange group of attendants and drivers: Turks, Greeks, and Armenians, middle eastern natives who were expert in handling these peculiar beasts. In command of the party was another oddity, considering the situation. He was a naval officer, Lieutenant Edward Fitzgerald Beale.

After service in the Mexican War, Beale had engaged in American desert exploration. Currently he was on leave from his position as superintendent of Indian affairs in California and Nevada to conduct an experiment in camel transportation across the southwestern deserts of the United States.

With the caravan rode Captain Lee and his family, returning from leave. For them the trip had been much more tragic than fascinating.

Beale had made himself thoroughly familiar with the problems of travel in the Southwest. The purpose of his expedition was to examine the endurance of the camels and their capability for providing transportation across these wastelands, especially for the army. The idea had been put to this test by Secretary of War Jefferson Davis, who had been impressed with suggestions made by certain army officers. Davis persuaded Congress to appropriate $30,000 for the camel experiment. The first of these animals shipped from the Near East arrived at Indianola, Texas, in 1856. They were brought inland to a permanent camp and staging area at Val Verde, sixty miles northwest of San Antonio.

The caravan that lumbered into Fort Davis had left Val Verde on June 26, 1857, and had covered the 475 miles to Fort Davis in twenty-two days.[49]

On July 2 at Fort Clark, an important outpost on the road from San Antonio, Captain Lee had stopped to rest during a return trip to Fort Davis from vacation in eastern Texas. He was accompanied by his wife, Margaret; his six-year-old daughter, Katherine; a fifteen-month-old son, Arthur; and a mounted guard of fifteen soldiers. When Lee and his party came upon the camel train bound also for Fort Davis they joined it for the rest of the journey. The combined force would provide better protection against Indian attack.

But life on this wild frontier could hold many other unexpected hazards. One concerned health, and any sort of medical care was often hundreds of miles away. The Lees' young son fell ill and became worse as each day passed, despite what would have been solicitous attention from his parents and apparently from other members of the party. On July 9 the boy died just as the motley group of wagons, horses, mules, camels, and their masters reached Fort Lancaster on the way to Davis. May Humphreys Stacey, a nineteen-year-old Pennsylvanian serving as one of three assistants to U.S. Navy Lieutenant Beale, described the tragedy:

> This afternoon a very melancholy fact was communicated to us. Captain Lee, the officer . . . who had traveled with us from Fort Clark

[49] May Humphreys Stacey, *Uncle Sam's Camels: The Journal of May Humphreys Stacey, Supplemented by the Report of Edward Fitzgerald Beale*, ed. Lewis Burt Lesley (Cambridge, Mass.: Harvard University Press, 1929), pp. 6, 11.

where we met him, had the misfortune to lose his little son fifteen months old. This poor, little fellow had been unwell for several days, gradually growing worse each day, notwithstanding our efforts to relieve him. The Captain had hardly reached the post before the mournful event occurred. We were all very sorry and sympathized deeply with the Captain and his poor wife. For her our sympathy was particularly lively. There she was in the wilderness at a frontier post, with only one or two of her own sex, and they entire strangers. . . .[50]

Lieutenant Beale wrote in his own diary how deeply concerned he and his men were about the fate of the child who had lingered at the point of death for several days.[51] The entire party stayed over a day or two at Fort Lancaster to attend the funeral service conducted in that lonesome land.

If the death affected companions of the trail to such an extent, it certainly must have left a heavy mark on the family, although Lee apparently wrote nothing about it. The fifteen-month-old who had died was the second son the Lees had lost. Another, William, had died several years earlier at a young age. Later, a third son, Henry, would die at the age of seven (on February 9, 1868) while the Lees were visiting in Rochester, New York. A newspaper account at that time would give the cause of death as "an affection of the brain."[52]

Lee's short association with camels on the San Antonio–El Paso road in July, 1857, was not his only encounter with these animals. A year and one-half later he was involved in a camel experiment of his own. In the spring of 1859 he commanded C and D companies of the Eighth Infantry on a march from Fort Hudson, on Devil's River, to a spot designated for a military camp on the Rio Frio below Fort Inge. His force was instructed to determine the endurance required of foot troops in following the long-loping animals.

Years later Lee related an anecdote recalled from those days:

"I say, stranger! what air them things a comin' along thar?" was a question asked of an officer, by one of a squad of mounted herders, assembled on the road, in the vicinity of Fort Inge. . . . If the herder was curious, the animals on which his party were mounted showed symptoms both of curiosity and alarm.

"They are camels, and you had better get your horses out of the way, or you will have exercise," was the reply.

"Exercise, h——! they can stand it if we can, I reckon."

Ding, dong! ding, dong! The sound of the camels' bells reached the horses' ears, when they manifested signs of sitting down on their hind-quarters, and commenced sparring at the clouds; but when the scent of the animals came down upon the breeze, there was such a convulsion of horseflesh as those riders had not been prepared for, and the different directions those quadrupeds took, and the speed they displayed in manifesting their inclinations to get out of sight, made it doubtful in the minds of the lookers on, if they should ever again come together; and it took but a fleeting moment to make that plain lonesome and "sparse," as the "crackers" say, of Texan cavaliers.

Ding, dong! ding, dong! and the caravan moved on, exhibiting no outward signs of any knowledge of the wild stampede it had created.[53]

Although most of the camel tests proved satisfactory at first, the situation changed. Summer came, accompanied by a long drought, hot winds, and sandstorms. Earth moisture disappeared. "The ground cracked open and a hard-baked crust formed on the surface. . . . Then . . . teams began to pass a caravan on the road, the camels . . . resting upon their leathery knees. . . . The drivers began to look anxious, then dubious, then disgusted." The experiment ended in failure. "From Texas to Arizona, the small sharp igneous rocks had literally cut to shreds the soft, padded feet of the camels."[54]

Captain Lee's own conclusions were made from an artist's view.

[50] Ibid., p. 57.
[51] Ibid., p. 158.
[52] Rochester, N.Y., *Union and Advertiser*, February 10, 1868.

[53] Lee, "Reminiscences," II, 370–371.
[54] Raht, *Romance of Davis Mountains*, pp. 139, 370.

He said, "Camel caravans, however picturesque and imposing they may . . . appear to the traveller's eye on eastern deserts, were not beautiful to the beholder on the wild plains of Texas. Tent poles, camp kettles, and other . . . [army] paraphernalia . . . however useful, are not ornamental in any position; [and] when distributed indiscriminately on the humps of camels, they are simply hideous."[55]

[55] Lee, "Reminiscences," II, 369–370.

On the Mexican Border

LEE's checkered tour of duty at Fort Davis had ended. He had been detached even before conducting that camel experiment. In September, 1858, he had left Davis in command of two infantry companies with orders to establish what would become Fort Quitman.

Lee himself commented on the good fortune of his transfer out from under the supervision of an unfriendly superior officer: "'As the temperaments, and prevailing notions of the head of the Eighth [Colonel Seawell], and the commander of Company 'C' [Lee], did not at all times travel in harmony, there was a mutual feeling of relief, when separation was ordered from the Headquarters of the Department.'"[56]

Fort Quitman was to be located 120 miles west, on the Rio Grande, some 80 miles downriver from the town named Franklin, which changed its name to El Paso about that time.[57] Quitman would serve as another outpost guarding the long trail to California.

After receiving the orders to establish the new post, Lee realized he faced a difficult task. He foresaw two major problems. First, how could he safely, efficiently, and most comfortably move his company of fifty to sixty foot soldiers and numerous army families (including his own) across 120 miles of rough desert country with temperatures that easily matched the harshness of the surrounding desolation? The second problem, which could be put out of mind until later, regarded planning and building a fort in an area almost unknown to him.

[56] Ibid., p. 367.
[57] Webb, *Handbook of Texas*, I, 561.

Lee mused over his immediate prospects. He had available for the trip four rickety wagons and an inadequate supply of casks for carrying water. Worse, a two-month drought had dried springs and mudholes he might ordinarily expect to find along the way. But he commenced the journey, and he later described its perils and privations:

> The sufferings of the command during the six days of that wearisome march, from excessive heat, and want of water, was almost beyond endurance. The sighs and moanings of women, and the cries of young children, parching and panting for lack of the cooling element, was heart rending. For long, mid-day hours the command was compelled to lie motionless, under the blistering rays of the sun, in consequence of the utter exhaustion of the animals, and their inability to proceed with their over laden wagons, one of which had broken down, on the second day out.[58]

When Lee arrived at the site of the post-to-be he confronted the second major problem—that of building a fort where materials were scarce. Good wood was especially hard to find. Fortunately, however, Rio Grande mud and gravel could make sturdy adobe buildings and enclosures, and Fort Quitman appeared as a reality in a surprisingly short time. Searches of surrounding territory—including secret forays into Mexican river bottoms—even yielded enough good timber joists to be used in construction. When completed, the fort aroused the admiration of area residents.

[58] Lee, "Reminiscences," II, 368.

Years later Lee concluded his reminiscences of Fort Quitman with notable finality:

> Whether the rains of heaven have long since washed away all traces of its own towering flag staff, and lime washed walls, or if it still exists, the admiration of wandering mescaleros and overland stage drivers, is matter of small interest to any one, and so—
> We'll banish it from memory if we can,
> And bid a long farewell to Fort Quitman.[59]

After the camel experiment, Captain Lee's next significant military involvement came in a series of border skirmishes known as the "Cortinas Wars," although Lee himself saw little or no action in that fighting and obviously looked upon the entire conflict as something more worthy of opéra bouffe. Participants in the Cortinas Wars were less amused.

In September, 1859, a charismatic Mexican rancher named Juan Nepomuceno Cortina (or Cortinas) and a large group of followers, apparently angered at Anglo-American injustices to Mexican-Americans and distrustful of the American law to protect their rights, entered Brownsville, Texas, shot four men, released all the prisoners from the jail, and held the town. They were finally persuaded to leave by some of the leading citizens of Matamoros, Mexico. In the next two months, after retreating to his ranch on the north side of the Rio Grande a few miles west of Brownsville, Cortina and his men repelled the attacks of the combined militias of Brownsville and Matamoros and later of a force of Texas Rangers under Captain W. G. Tobin.

At the request of the citizens of Brownsville, the U.S. Army moved in. General D. E. Twiggs, commander of the Eighth Military Department, ordered 165 regulars under Major S. P. Heintzelman to reoccupy Fort Brown. On December 27, 1859, strengthened by a force of 120 Rangers, they met Cortina's army in battle at Rio Grande City. Sixty of Cortina's men died, but no Anglo-Americans were killed.

Little more than a month later Cortina was eliminated as a border threat when a Ranger force led by Major John S. ("Rip") Ford attacked him just as he was apparently seeking to capture the Rio Grande steamboat *Ranchero*. Cortina retreated into the Burgos Mountains of Mexico. A new Eighth Military Department commander, Colonel Robert E. Lee, arrived on the scene with more soldiers, and the Cortinas Wars were over.[60]

Arthur Lee, no apparent kin to the colonel who would soon earn fame as the great Confederate commander of the Civil War, arrived about the same time—too late to see any real action. When Arthur Lee heard about the "invasion" of the country around Brownsville he was probably at Fort Stockton in December, 1859. Early in the following February he and C Company, along with other infantry units, encamped near Laredo, having been ordered there for the supposedly ensuing campaign. Soon after arriving in Laredo, Lee received a letter from Major Heintzelman at Fort Brown: "I have just received an express that Mexicans fired upon the Steamboat Ranchero at La Bahia 35 miles above here; also upon Capt. Ford's Rangers, wounding one of the latter mortally. He crossed over with his whole command and drove the Mexicans back. Captain Stoneman's company of cavalry is advancing to support him. I will be pleased to be joined by two of the companies of your command at the earliest moment. At Ringgold Barracks are two 24 pdr. Howitzers I wish brought down by the troops."[61] Unfortunately, records apparently do not exist revealing details of Lee's part in the rest of the campaign. It is obvious, how-

[59] Ibid., p. 369.

[60] Walter Prescott Webb, *The Texas Rangers*, rev. ed. (Austin: University of Texas Press, 1965), p. 176; Webb, *Handbook of Texas*, I, 417.

[61] Original letter dated February 4, 1860, at Fort Brown, Texas, in the library of the Rochester Museum and Science Center, Rochester, N.Y.

ever, that by the time he reached his destination the situation had calmed.

From his allusions to the Cortinas Wars it is evident that Lee looked upon the fighting as more ludicrous than serious. He showed scant respect or sympathy for people caught up in this and other conflicts when he wrote:

> The ordinary manner of carrying on a siege against any of the frontier towns, is to muster a herd of a few hundred "greasers," and dividing it into smaller herds, take possession of the roads and trails leading to and from the interior, and raise the revolutionary *rag*. This of course cuts off the supply of *carne*, upon the daily reception of which, the people are almost entirely dependent. They can subsist for a short time on *chili colorado*, but it is not a food calculated to make muscle, or lively as it is, to keep up the spirits for any length of time.
>
> On occasions when the besieged are unusually stubborn—from an excess of loyalty, or in consequence of an unusual supply on hand of *frijoles*—exchanges are made between the besiegers and the besieged, through a white flag, in which *frijoles* are swapped for *carne*. But as the latter, in the hands of the outsiders, is inexhaustible, and as the former are always too limited to hold out long, the consequence is that the town must eventually "knock under," or as is generally the case, rake together a few hundred *pesos*, and buy the besiegers off.
>
> The raising of the siege is followed by a grand *baile*, in which friends and foes alike mingle, exchange congratulations, and wash out all memory of past hotilities in soothing anisette and soul stirring *agua[r]diente*.[62]

More of Lee's cynicism is evident in a bit of his poetry, a fourteen-stanza ballad entitled, "The Rout of the Black Cortina: A Legend of the 'Rio Bravo del Norte,'" which pokes some fun, too, at the U.S. Army. Some excerpts follow; the piece appeared in entirety in "Reminiscences of the Regiment."

[62] Lee, "Reminiscences," II, 406–407.

The Heintzelman, five hundred strong,
    Fresh from the land of doodle dandy;
With Texan Rangers, five miles long,
    Came sweeping up the Rio Grande.

And gaily rode the Heintzelman,
    Not he of fear or death e'er dreaming;
Rode proudly as the Ritter Ban,
    With trumpet blast, and banners streaming.
        Vive Americana!

And combat burned in every eye,
    And brows were flushed as red verbena;
Whilst loud and wild arose the cry
    Of "Vengeance on the Black Cortina."
        Hi! hi!

The Heintzelman his sabre drew,
    Drew Captain Ford his old revolver;
Cried King, "Charge on my boys in blue,
    And give the devils a dissolver."

"Call in the guides;" the guides were called,
    Bad samples of the Texan Ranger;
For they through chaparral had crawled,
    Back to the rear, and out of danger.

The Heintzelman, he swore a swear,
    A mighty swear; we'll not repeat it;
But H-r-y when he tears his hair,
    And stamps the bunch grass, could not beat it.
        Maldijos, caramba!

The Heintzelman, he flashed his blade,
    The red legs held their brass guns handy;
The Rangers yelled out "who's afraid?"

As they swept up the Rio Grande.
 Vamos, pasearse, hi!

Now where are they, and where is he,
 The "hijo" of the "gentefina?"
A fearless Ranger climbs a tree,
 And spies afar the Black Cortina.
  Bueno, Muchacho!

Now ruthless robber, hold thy best,
 Or vengeance dire will quick confound thee;
No soft arms circle now thy breast,
 The Heintzelman is all around thee.
  Flash, bang, whiz!

Roared out the guns, the sabres flashed,
 To right and left the horsemen thundered;
The gravel flew, the chaparral crashed,
 That was the charge where no one blundered.
  "Bravos, los Americanos!"

They waver now, and see they fly,
 The day is ours, their lines are broken;
But where's the Black Cortina? hi!
 Alas! he's gone, and left no token.[63]
  . . .

[63] Ibid., pp. 403–405.

Lee and the Indians

ARTHUR LEE'S principal adversaries over the years were not Cortina and any number of other Mexicans. They were, instead, the North American Indians who barred the way to "progress" and the filling out of a continent. Lee had fought Seminoles in Florida and had helped to move the Winnebagos out of northern areas. Now, during his long tour of duty in Texas, he became well acquainted with still other tribes: Comanches, Lipan Apaches, and Kiowas. A close look at his association with, and his attitude toward, Indians shows a sympathy for their plight—one shared in those days by some other military men who nevertheless obeyed orders, like Lee, and helped to sweep the western wilderness clean of the pesky red men who had inhabited that area for centuries.

Lee seems to have had more familiarity with Comanches during his first four years in Texas, 1848–1852. From the fall of 1849 until early spring of 1852 his activities centered around the area of Fort Croghan, located in Comanche country sixty miles northwest of Austin.[64] The officers' quarters there were four houses, each having two rooms separated by a hall, roofed with oak shingles, and squared or faced with common log kitchens. Lee, however, owned a private home on land nearby that he had purchased.[65] This arrangement surely would have improved his living conditions, which were usually primitive at such frontier posts. The privacy also would have been beneficial to his sketching.

A charming watercolor remains as a pictorial record of Lee's early association with Indians at Fort Croghan (Plate 4). It shows three cone-shaped hills in the background, a coniferous tree in the foreground, and near the tree a group of Indians. Two of the men are on foot, holding lances; a third is mounted on a mule. Also shown in the same scene are two Indian women with three children.

At least two other watercolors probably from this same period depict not Fort Croghan, but other scenes. One is a view on the Guadalupe River, where Lee and his men had encamped early in 1849 while on their way to Camp (not Fort) Worth (Plate 1). In the undated picture high bluffs tower over the figures of men fishing in the distance. The other scene is a view of the Brazos River near Fort Graham, where Lee was on detached service for a time in early 1851 (Plate 5).[66] Two horsemen and a pack mule are shown crossing the river near the fort.

Most of Lee's first four years in Texas, however, centered around Fort Croghan, which he commanded from time to time. In those early years in Texas he showed a sympathy for his foes, the Indians, that he had revealed in earlier campaigns elsewhere and in some of his poems. Later he wrote:

> Whether or not the Comanches, Wichitas, Lipans, Kiawas [sic], and the other wild tribes of the Texas mountains and prairies, were more docile, and less inclined to toy with human top knots then, than now, certain it is, that Indian outrages were few and far between in those

---

[64] Fort Croghan Post Returns, 1849–1852, Record Group 94, Microcopy 617 (1965), Roll 70, National Archives, Washington, D.C.

[65] Deed, Peter Kerr to J. F. Proctor, October 15, 1855, in Deed Records, Burnet County, Texas. Copy provided by Thomas C. Ferguson, Burnet, Texas.

[66] Fort Croghan Post Returns, 1849–1852, Record Group 94, Microcopy 617 (1965), Roll 70, National Archives, Washington, D.C.

days, notwithstanding the frequent advent among them of certain Government officials, who made "promises to the ear to break them to the heart," and wearied them with such drivelling, and mouthy talks, as would have made christian white men swear, if not, under the circumstances, steal. When Indian agents deal out, as annuities or presents from the Government, such articles as jackplanes, fiddles, wash-basins, tooth-brushes, back-combs, and *unmentionable crockery-ware*—the cleanings out of a miscellaneous backwood's country store—to the red children of the Great Father, it is rather calculated to shake their faith in the good sense, if not the honesty of their white brother.[67]

In a footnote to this passage Lee commented: "There is no exaggeration in this allusion. Such an issue was actually made on the San Saba River in 1850 or 1851, and the writer witnessed the exchange of a large number of the articles mentioned, with an army sutler, for the consideration of a few pounds of sugar and tobacco."[68] The incident must have made a great impression on Lee, for in a comic ballad published in the 1870s he again describes the unwanted and unusable goods doled out to a disgruntled Indian and his daughter by the agent:

> From the vale of the San Saba,
>   for some sixty miles or more
> He had journeyed on the prairies to
>   surprise a trader's store.
> He had various utensils,
>   swinging on the backs of mules,
> Such as jack planes, augers, handsaws,
>   gimlets, squares and other tools,
> And a various assortment of such wares,
>   for sale and show,
> As are found in backwoods country stores
>   whose stock is running low

> And these were of the offerings
>   of that Indian Agent man
> With his herd of long horned cattle and
>   his oxcart caravan.

> It was plain to all beholders
>   that this chief on traffic bent,
> Had more of wrath than kindness
>   within his bosom pent;
> Beside him rode his daughter,
>   dark-eyed princess of the band,
> With unmentionable crockery,
>   a sample in each hand.
> And disappointment rode the brows
>   of all that band of reds:
> No blanket graced their tawny backs,
>   no trinkets decked their heads.[69]

Of the seventy poems included in Lee's book *Army Ballads*, five are on Indian subjects and several others mention Indians. With only one exception (a piece entitled "Saniho") all of them extol Indian virtues and focus on the tragedy of Indian culture swept away by white civilization. Typical is "About the Chief Hotulka":

> His wampum on the cypress hung;
> To which dark flesh and ringlet clung;
> Torn from the brows of dying men,
> Midst shouts he ne'er would hear again . . .
> They come, they come like ocean waves;
> For fifty years these feet have pressed
> The grassless earth of white men's graves,
> And yet they come, no rest, no rest. . . .[70]

Such sympathetic understanding might seem strange for an

---

[67] Lee, "Reminiscences," II, 344–345.
[68] Ibid., p. 345n.

[69] "Ye Representative Indian Agent," clipping in scrapbook, Arthur T. Lee Papers, Rush Rhees Library, University of Rochester, N.Y.
[70] Arthur T. Lee, *Army Ballads and Other Poems* (1871), p. 32.

army man during the Indian wars. Stranger yet, Lee could be, and had been, harsh with those Indian foe-friends. Years earlier, after the Seminole Chief Waxihadjo had murdered an express rider carrying the mail, Lee pursued the man, captured him, and had him hanged. Despite his experience with Indian savagery, however, Lee always had a strong sense of the injustice Indians suffered at the hands of white men, and he retained it during his Texas tour. Answering an inquiry from Major George T. Howard, Indian agent for West Texas, Captain Lee wrote:

> For three years I have been in almost daily intercourse with the [Comanche] bands of Buffalo Hump, Yellow Wolf, [Katumse], and [Sanaco], and, on all occasions, found them friendly and well-disposed toward the whites, provided they were in any way supplied with food to sustain life.
> For a trifling expense to the government, it could insure the safety of the frontier. Troops have moved into the heart, if not beyond the limits of their hunting ground. They want a country set apart for them. I would further state that they will be compelled to resort to plunder for the necessities of life as there is a great scarcity of game in the country to which they are now restricted.[71]

Obviously, then, Lee preferred sketching Indians to shooting them. One of his most interesting drawings is a rear view of Sanaco showing him wearing a brilliant blue garment with an orange top and holding a long lance (Plate 24). In the foreground appears a well-dressed, barefoot, light-complexioned woman holding her hand on the neck of a donkey she is leading. She is wearing a somewhat Mexican-looking dress and appears to be mestiza rather than pure Indian.

[71] Lee to Howard, March 15, 1852, in University of Texas Library Archives, Austin.

(Probably she was Sanaco's wife. Many Southern Comanche men had Mexican wives captured in raids.) Behind the woman is a boy three or four years old. A small dog in the foreground completes the scene.

Yellow Wolf, also mentioned favorably in the letter to Major Howard, apparently became Lee's very good friend. Lee painted Yellow Wolf's portrait in oils (Plate 58). In it the Indian is seen wearing a shell earring in his left ear. Later, Yellow Wolf gave this jewelry piece to Lee, and eventually Lee's granddaughter presented it to the Rochester Museum and Science Center along with the painting.

Another Lee picture of Yellow Wolf exists somewhere. It is a small watercolor sketch signed in pencil, "A. T. Lee pinxit," and dated "20 Apr. 1857" which was offered for sale in New York City in 1954; its eventual owner has never been traced.[72] That April of 1857 Lee was stationed at Fort Davis, but on the twentieth of the month he was on leave and might have encountered the Comanche chief somewhere. It is possible that the oil portrait now owned by the Rochester Museum was painted later, based on the watercolor field sketch.

Also existent is an ink sketch showing Yellow Wolf in three poses, apparently drawn by that chief himself as a primitive self-portrait. Family tradition has it that Yellow Wolf gave this drawing to Lee. It also shows a horse and a row of rifles opposing a line of arrows sketched on the opposite side of the sheet, possibly representing some of the "coups" achieved by Yellow Wolf. Captain Lee was a friend, however, and not a coup.

[72] The catalog of Argosy Book Stores, New York City, listed this sketch as its property in March, 1954. No record of an eventual buyer exists.

Civil War and Last Years

ANOTHER tragedy was coming, too, and this one would engulf white men. Nowhere in his "Reminiscences" or any extant articles, however, did Arthur Lee mention forebodings of the Civil War.

That conflict was looming ever higher on the political horizon after the "Cortinas Wars" had ended, with Lee having taken virtually no active part in them. He and his soldiers, along with other infantry companies, arrived at Fort Brown on February 27, 1860, and remained there until March 29, but Cortinas had fled.

Lee had been in the vicinity of Fort Brown earlier, of course, but possibly this five-week sojourn, as quiet as it must have been, gave him time to add to his sketchbook. The Rochester Museum and Science Center now holds a sketch of Brownsville, and in the album now kept by the Rochester Historical Society is a watercolor sketch of Matamoros, Mexico, just across the Rio Grande river (Plates 26, 27). From Fort Brown, Lee and his C Company men were ordered to Ringgold Barracks, where they arrived on April 3, 1860, and stayed seven months. From there they marched 587 miles northwest to Fort Stockton, a new post (built of adobe) erected for additional protection of the San Antonio–El Paso stage route.[73]

Lee and his family remained at Fort Stockton until early April, 1861, a week or so before Confederate forces fired on Fort Sumter, in Charleston Harbor, to begin the Civil War on April 14. The Lees were living at Fort Stockton, in fact, when Lee made his first reference to the war that would soon divide his nation. He mentioned some "traitorous" remarks of General David E. Twiggs, headquar-

tered in San Antonio. Still, most officers loyal to the Union apparently believed that when war came they would be allowed to march to the Gulf Coast with loyal troops and there be evacuated to a northern harbor.

Lee seemed to sense greater trouble. He arranged for his family to move to San Antonio; then, in early April, he left C Company in the command of Lieutenant E. W. H. Read and went ahead to San Antonio with the hope of expediting movement of his men through that city and on toward the coast and eventual evacuation. C Company left Fort Stockton on April 10 for its own march to San Antonio, via Fort Clark, and to the coast.

War overtook them all. "The first rebel rag that greeted the eyes of the officers and private soldiers of Company 'C,'" Lee wrote later, "floated from the flagstaff of Fort Clarke [sic] at the head of the Las Moras."[74] Lee hurried on from Fort Clark, still ahead of his company, bound for San Antonio and those arrangements he hoped to make. Even so, he reached San Antonio about the same time his company did and met with great disappointment. Lee recounted his experience later, in the third person:

> Arriving at midnight, he had no thought that either himself or his command, would be interrupted in their march to the coast. [But] . . . early morning found him a prisoner in close confinement, surrounded by a guard of armed rebels, who for personal safety, had taken post behind neighboring fences, and in adjoining [jacales].
>
> During the forenoon he was visited by an individual assuming to be

---

[73] Frazer, *Forts of the West*, p. 162.

[74] Lee, "Reminiscences," II, 415.

Major Duff, of the Confederate Lone Star, High Joint Commission, Committee of Public Safety, Texan Army, who informed him that his, the Captain's, company was in restraint on the main plaza, surrounded by Confederate troops; and that the members having refused to surrender their arms, were in imminent danger of annihilation, and needed his presence.

Permission having been demanded by the Captain, to see and consult with Colonel Waite, then commanding the United States troops in Texas, before he would act in the matter, it was granted; and at the close of a brief interview between the Colonel and the Captain, it was decided—as there seemed to be no other course left—to peaceably surrender the arms of the company, and await further developments.

That was a glorious sight for the people of a nation not at war (no blow had as yet been struck for or against rebellion)—the sight of a body of soldiers consisting of *less than thirty men*, reduced to the last round of ammunition, who had committed no offence against law or order; but on the contrary, had been for years—with their brother soldiers—toiling and pouring out their blood, on the wild prairies, and in the dark mountain gorges of the State, for the welfare and safety of its citizens, insulted and robbed in open day, by an armed and ammunitioned mob, thrice their numbers, covered by the shelter of adobe walls, and backed by a city of howling rebels. It was a glorious sight for free men.[75]

The date was April 21, 1861. Official documents carefully preserved by Lee's family indicate subsequent events. One paper, headed "Special Orders" and dated April 22 at San Antonio by Major S. Mackin, C.S.A., released Captain Lee from arrest with the provision that "He will not for the present do army duty for the United States" and that he would report in person on the following morning to the officer commanding Confederate troops. That next day Lee signed his parole (also preserved), stating that he would not take up arms against the Confederate government during the war and that he would not correspond with U.S. authorities giving information

against Confederate interests unless regularly exchanged. Still another document preserved to this day is an order signed by Major Mackin stating that Captain A. T. Lee—"the bearer," a prisoner of war on his parole of honor—had permission to pass through any of the Confederate States without hindrance or molestation.[76]

Lee and his family then commenced their long journey home. They must have reached the North within a few weeks of his release at San Antonio, because Lee was on court-martial duty at West Point by July, 1861. After that he was stationed for a while at Elmira, New York, on mustering and disbursing duty and as drillmaster.[77] Thus he abided by his promise not to bear arms against the Confederate States unless regularly exchanged. In October, 1861, he was promoted to major at the age of forty-seven, but still he could not fight.

About one year later his exchange was declared effective, on August 27, 1862, and he was free for combat duty. His military record shows that he commanded the Second Infantry Regiment of the V Army Corps and took part in the Battle of Gettysburg. There he was wounded in the right ankle and hip. His wounds kept him absent from duty until January 9, 1864, but soon after suffering them he was able to write from his field hospital a detailed description of the battle to Captain J. W. Ames, acting assistant adjutant general.[78]

Because of his poor health, no doubt, Lee was retired from active service on January 20, 1865.[79] During the next few years he made several extended visits to Rochester, New York, which would in time become his permanent residence. Lee was in the city on April 19,

[75] Ibid., pp. 417–419.

[76] Original documents in the library of the Rochester Museum and Science Center, Rochester, N.Y.

[77] Neil D. Cranmer, "Chemung County's Part in the Civil War," *Chemung Historical Journal* (Elmira, N.Y.), I, no. 1 (September, 1955): 7.

[78] *The War of the Rebellion: Compilation of the Official Records of the Union and Confederate Armies* (Washington, D.C.: War Department, 1880–1901), Series 2, XXVII, 646–647.

[79] Wilhelm, *Synopsis of the History of the Eighth U.S. Infantry*, p. 281.

1865, when the body of assassinated President Abraham Lincoln was brought by rail, and Lee had the distinction of being one of eight prominent persons named to serve as pallbearers for a public ceremony.[80] Appropriate recognition also came to Lee from the War Department: elevation to lieutenant colonel, retroactive to July 2, 1863. A Rochester newspaper carried this comment:

> It is stated in our exchanges that Major A. T. Lee of this city has been brevetted Lieut. Colonel in the Regular Army for gallant service at Gettysburg, Pa. July 2, 1863. . . . He has been more than twenty-five years in the public service of his country, and has, we believe, acquitted himself well and has performed a world of labor for the government. He was a Captain in Texas when the war broke out, was taken prisoner by the rebels of that state whom he had protected from deprivations, [was] despoiled of his property, paroled and sent north. In due time he was released from parole and resumed his place in the Army. At Gettysburg he was badly wounded, but, as soon as he recovered, entered upon the duty assigned him and has prosecuted it ever since. . . .[81]

Lee was eventually promoted to full colonel, with his commission dated July 28, 1868. The same Rochester newspaper printed a story about this promotion on February 6, 1869.

Meanwhile, Lee had not been employed since his retirement early in 1865. Two days after his promotion to full colonel, however, he received a civilian appointment as deputy governor of the new Soldiers' Home and Park recently established near the city of Washington. Records show that Lee helped to landscape the grounds, among other tasks.

The setting was picturesque. The Soldiers' Home had been located near Howard University on a commanding height of ground. Initially it served two hundred retired and invalid army men, providing "every possible convenience for soldiers in respect of heating, ventilating, bedding, cooking, bathing, reading, etc. . . . The soldiers like their life of ease and comfort and have the advantage of books, newspapers and religious instruction. They are not obliged to work but have compensation for light labor."[82]

Colonel Lee was elevated to the governorship of the Soldiers' Home in September, 1869. He retained that post until 1872, and apparently his three-year tenure brought him additional public appreciation. A reviewer of Lee's book of poetry, *Army Ballads*, wrote, "No one possessed of any feeling can drive of a sunny day through the Soldiers' Home without a feeling that a grand poem has been made all about him to beautify and adorn our common life. Colonel Lee has created out of slender means the Soldiers' Home, one of the sweetest spots in the world. . . ."[83]

A highlight of Lee's administration was the visit there of Prince Arthur, son of Queen Victoria, on January 26, 1870, but Lee and his family enjoyed many other opportunities to partake of the exciting Washington social life. Invitation cards preserved by Lee's granddaughter show that during the winters of 1870 and 1871 Colonel and Mrs. Lee were guests at social functions hosted by Secretary of State Hamilton Fish, Secretary of War William W. Belknap, Postmaster General John Creswell, and General William T. Sherman.[84]

The year 1871 was an especially productive one for Lee. In August his book *Army Ballads and Other Poems*—a small, cloth-bound volume of 160 pages containing seventy poems—was published. The book was dedicated to "General W. T. Sherman / and to / My Comrades of Many a Joyous Hour, Stolen from the / Vicissitudes of Frontier Life in Tent and Bivouac." Lee's romantic ballads echo the tones of Thomas Hood, Sir Walter Scott, and others. Twelve poems are on

---

[80] Rochester, N.Y., *Union and Advertiser*, April 20, 1865.
[81] Ibid., August 10, 1866.

[82] Newspaper clippings, undated and without source, in Kate Lee scrapbook, Arthur T. Lee Papers, Rush Rhees Library, University of Rochester, N.Y.
[83] Ibid.
[84] Ibid.

military themes, twelve are on death, seventeen are laments or regrets for lost youth, and five are on Indian subjects. For the book Lee also provided designs for three woodcut illustrations produced by J. W. Orr of New York City.

Two contemporary reviews of Lee's book were generally favorable. One appeared in a Washington newspaper. It described Lee as

> one of the best known and popular officers in the United States army. . . . He has a talent in song-writing which almost equals the readiness of an improvisation; he sings as another pure lyricist (Thomas Moore) did, with charming melody and expression; he has competent knowledge of music, and unlike Scott, Byron and Moore, and other poets exercises the pencil to illustrate the productions of his pen. . . . Colonel Lee's songs have been sung wherever the national banner has been carried. He has done for our army what Charles Dibden did for the British Navy.[85]

Another critic, unidentified, praised the poems, saying that they tell of events looked at by the soldier from an ideal point of view and contain choice words and "musical utterances of an active, outdoor life." This same reviewer indicated some regret that Lee had not included pieces about the Civil War, but he accounted for this "by remembering that our book is a hearty history written in an earlier day, when youth was in its glow and poetry its ordinary utterance."[86] Two years later the New York music publishers William Halls and Sons published a set of sheet music entitled "Clover Blossoms" that included a series of Lee's ballads set to music by Henry Tucker.[87]

More Lee poetry probably published in 1871 (but not in *Army Ballads*) appeared in newspapers as apparently unsolicited poetic contributions. These poems discussed such subjects as the evils of retirement for an army officer (signed with the name "Vandyke Brown," a Lee pseudonym) and man's sinful quest for gold and riches (signed "D'Or," another pseudonym). Lee's most important literary creation, however, was his "Reminiscences of the Regiment" —the 367-page contribution that appeared as part of a history of the Eighth Infantry during that same productive year of 1871.

In 1872, following relinquishment of the post of governor of the Soldiers' Home, Colonel Lee and his wife established permanent residence in Rochester. Lee had several reasons for choosing that city. He had known it over a long period. In 1843, as a second lieutenant, he had spent several months in Rochester. Later, he had been stationed (as a recruiting officer) there from early fall of 1846 to the spring of 1848, when he had sailed for Vera Cruz, Mexico. Years later he wrote his recollections of that stay in Rochester; the article appeared in a city newspaper in 1870 under the heading, "'Then/Now' by An Ex-Lieutenant." Another reason for his choice of Rochester as a residence was the fact that his daughter Kate had married William J. Ashley, a Rochester banker. During the remaining seven years of Lee's life—from 1872 to 1879—he spent fall, winter, and spring in the city. Every summer he moved to Shelter Island, New York, where he obviously devoted much time to painting. Several watercolor sketches of Shelter Island scenery are included in the Lee picture collection at the Rush Rhees Library of the University of Rochester.

Lee's health seems to have been reasonably good until near the end of his life. One of two existing obituaries of him stated, "He returned here [Rochester] seriously but not hopelessly ill. . . . Alarming symptoms, however, developed . . . Sunday [December 28, 1879] . . . [and] he passed away peacefully and resignedly [the next morning]."[88] He lies buried in the Ashley family plot, Mount Hope Cemetery, Rochester.

An editor of the Rochester *Democrat & Chronicle* wrote (in the edition of December 30, 1879) a final paragraph of praise:

[85] Ibid.
[86] Ibid.
[87] Rochester, N.Y., *Union-Advertiser*, June 9, 1873.

[88] Rochester, N.Y., *Democrat & Chronicle*, December 30, 1879.

The death of Colonel Arthur T. Lee, which occurred in this city early yesterday morning will cause wide-spread sorrow; for he was a man well known to many of the best and most refined circles of the country and wherever he was known, he was loved for his manly traits and social graces. He was a typical army officer of the old school—elegant in person, chivalric in his bearing, engaging in conversation; but, he was also, something more than this. He was a man of scholarly tastes and of artistic accomplishments, and above all, he was the soul of honor, faithful to his promises, loyal to his friends and devoted to his family. . . . he was a whole-souled man, who leaves behind him a precious memory.

Lee the Artist

THE writer of one of Arthur T. Lee's obituaries mentioned Lee's interest in painting that apparently blossomed after he had completed his academic education.

> Developing a taste for art he went when quite a young man to Philadelphia and studied under Otis and Sully. His skill had prompt and generous recognition and he painted some 100 pieces, mostly portraits, some of them being of men very prominent in society and in politics—the governor of the State [Pennsylvania] among the number. Although deflected from art as a pursuit, Colonel Lee continued it as a recreation through life, in later years painting almost entirely in watercolors. There are numerous specimens of his brush in existence, including landscapes and marine views, and scenes in army life.[89]

A search of Philadelphia street directories of the period, however, reveals no trace of Lee. Records of the Pennsylvania Historical Society contain nothing about his early life.

In judging Lee as an artist it is frustrating that we are prevented from reviewing a wider range of his work, especially considering the oil portraits credited to him. Apparently the only oil that survives is that single portrait of Comanche Chief Yellow Wolf. It is a competent work even more photographic and representational than many of George Catlin's Indian pictures.

Probably many of Lee's pictures were based on field pencil sketches and were later worked into finished watercolors during his retirement years. But whenever he completed them, he obviously gave each one his careful attention. He was much concerned with composition, and he delighted in the picturesque. His pale tints and occasionally washed-out colors may be partially due to the fading of original pigments.

Probably more than sixty-five artists—some resident, others visiting—produced pictures of Texas during the last century. Only forty-two of the sixty-five could have been contemporary with Arthur Lee, and very few of them painted scenes in the same localities as did Lee. Some who did so were John Russell Bartlett, Seth Eastman, Henry C. Pratt, Carl Schuchard, Arthur Schott, and John E. Weyss.[90]

The work of Seth Eastman (1808–1875), another army officer, is closest to Lee's in style. That distinguished soldier-artist, who once taught topographical drawing at the United States Military Academy, is now considered one of the best portrayers of the American Indian. Although Eastman was in Texas from 1848 to 1849 and from 1855 to 1856, he was not where Lee was during those periods. Earlier, however, the two men had been at Fort Snelling, Minnesota, at the same time during the summer of 1848. They probably knew each other and might have gone on sketching trips together.

Possibly, too, Eastman actually influenced Lee. Some of Lee's Indian sketches seem to be very similar to Indian scenes sketched by Eastman and later worked into engravings used in Schoolcraft's *Indian Tribes of the United States*. Eastman's influence might have ap-

[89] Rochester, N.Y., *Union-Advertiser*, December 30, 1879.

[90] Pauline A. Pinckney, *Painting in Texas: The Nineteenth Century* (Austin: University of Texas Press, for the Amon Carter Museum of Western Art, Fort Worth, Texas, 1967).

peared also in Lee's "Fort Snelling" (Plate 39), "Falls of the Saint Anthony" (Plate 34), and "Minnehaha Falls" (Plate 35).

Other artists appear to have influenced Lee. Two of his pictures, in particular, are copied from the work of others. One (Plate 51), a well-executed scene of the Military Plaza in San Antonio, is similar to an engraving based on an original sketch by Arthur Schott (1813–1875), first assistant to Major William H. Emory, who was chief surveyor of the Mexico–United States Boundary Survey.[91]

Another (Plate 57) is a view of Brownsville, Texas, for which Lee obviously was indebted to boundary survey artist John E. Weyss (ca. 1820–1903). Weyss's and Lee's pictures of the scene are almost identical except for objects in the foreground.[92] Lee might have been a copier in some cases, but he was simply following a not uncommon practice of other nineteenth-century artists.

Because there is a sufficient variety of topics covered in Lee's watercolor sketches of Texas, they have importance as unique documents giving the flavor of the frontier. From them we get a feeling for terrain, topography, vegetation, and climate. Fortunately, there are enough human figures to give us also insight into life on the trail and into army encampments, Indians, and towns.

Lee made a significant contribution as a keenly observing artist, and his drawings are supplemented by his writings. He obviously wanted people then and later to have a true picture of the real Texas, a part of the West that lured those thousands of opportunity-seekers toward the setting sun so long ago. This book will, it is hoped, attest to his success.

[91] William H. Emory, *Report on the United States and Mexican Boundary Survey*, 34th Cong., 1st sess., 1857, House Exec. Doc. 135, II, frontispiece. The engraving is reprinted in Pinckney, *Painting in Texas*, p. 161.

[92] Emory, *Report on the United States and Mexican Boundary Survey*, I, 60. The engraving is reprinted in Pinckney, *Painting in Texas*, p. 165.

Fort Davis and Other Texas Paintings

T<small>HE</small> frontispiece and the twenty-seven other watercolors reproduced in the following section in their original sizes are scenes of Fort Davis and other locations in Texas as they appeared during Arthur T. Lee's years there. They were probably painted during his retirement from field sketches or finished pencil drawings much like the one of Fort Davis, Plate 19, in this section.

The paintings furnished by the Rochester Historical Society are included in a portfolio album of thirty casebound sheets. The paintings held by the Rochester Museum and Science Center, the Rush Rhees Library, and Kennedy Galleries, Inc., are loose sheets, some of which may once have been mounted in similar albums.

1. Guadalupe River

38

39

2. San Antonio, Texas

3. Alamo, San Antonio

42

43

4. View near Fort Croghan

45

5. Rio Brazos, Texas

47

6. Rio Grande City

7. Old Catholic Mission, Rio Grande

51

8. Upper Rio Grande

53

9. Sierra Prieta (Black Mountain), Texas

10. In Wild Rose Pass

11. Fort Davis, Texas

12. Canyon, Fort Davis—1

13. Fort Davis Scene—1

63

14. Maggie's Kitchen, Fort Davis

65

15. Canyon, Fort Davis—2

16. Charley's Kitchen, Fort Davis

17. Rocks above Fort Davis

70

18. Fort Davis Scene—2

72

19. Fort Davis

75

20. Overland Mail Station

21. Wolf Canyon, Texas

22. Wolf Canyon Water Hole

23. Comanche Lookout

83

24. Sanaho (Sanaco), a Comanche Chief

25. Guadalupe Peak

26. Brownsville, Texas

89

27. Matamoros, Mexico

28. Buffalo Hunt

Other Paintings by Arthur T. Lee

THIS section contains Lee's paintings of the Upper Mississippi River region, which he visited while participating in the removal of the Winnebago Indians, as well as two watercolor sketches of Mexico during the Mexican War and other western scenes. Also included is the portrait of Comanche Chief Yellow Wolf, the only oil portrait by Lee known to exist (Plate 58), and the two watercolors probably copied from engravings in the report of the United States–Mexican boundary survey (Plates 51, 57).

29. Upper Mississippi—1 (7 × 5⅛)

31. Mississippi near Crow Wing River (7⅝ × 4⅞)

30. Sioux Women Gambling (6⅞ × 4¼)

32. Chippewa Camp, Minnesota (7½ × 4⅞)

97

33. Indian Burial Place, Minnesota (7⅜ × 4½)

34. Falls of St. Anthony in 1848 (7¾ × 4½)

35. Minnehaha Falls, 1848 (4¼ × 5)

98

36. Lovers Leap on Lake Pepin, Mississippi River (7 × 4½)

38. Upper Mississippi River Scene—1 (6⅞ × 4¼)

37. Chippewas, Minnesota (5⅛ × 3¾)

39. Fort Snelling, Upper Mississippi (7 × 4⅛)

99

40. Upper Mississippi River Scene—2 (10⅞ × 6⅜)

42. Upper Mississippi River Scene—3 (7⅝ × 5)

41. Western Scene (11⅞ × 8)

43. Upper Mississippi—2 (6⅞ × 4⅜)

44. Upper Mississippi—3 (7⅛ × 4½)

46. Upper Mississippi River Scene—4 (7½ × 4⅜)

45. Upper Mississippi—4 (7⅜ × 4⅜)

47. Upper Mississippi River Scene—5 (7 × 4⅜)

48. Plains of Colorado (9¼ × 5⅝)

49. Near Vera Cruz, Mexico (6⅞ × 5⅛)

50. City of Mexico from Tuacubia (Tacubaya?) (10⅜ × 7)

51. Military Plaza, San Antonio (8¼ × 6¼)

102

52. Western Landscape (9¾ × 6¾)

54. Fort Riley or Fort Leavenworth, Kansas (8¾ × 5½)

53. Herd of Deer (10 × 7)

55. Wolf Canyon (7 × 7¾)

103

56. Indians Hunting Buffalo (10 × 7)

57. Brownsville, Texas (7⅞ × 5¼)

58. Portrait of Yellow Wolf (11¼ × 21)

104

Bibliography

Primary Sources

Manuscripts

Austin, Texas. University of Texas Library. Barker Texas History Center. U.S. Office of Indian Affairs Letters 1838–1862. Captain Arthur T. Lee to Major George T. Howard, March 15, 1852.

Bliss, Zenas Randall. "Reminiscences of Zenas R. Bliss, Major General United States Army." Typescript copy in University of Texas Library Archives, Austin.

Burnet County, Texas. Deed Records. Deed, Peter Kerr to J. F. Proctor, October 15, 1855.

Rochester, N.Y. Rochester Museum and Science Center. Arthur T. Lee papers.

———. Rush Rhees Library, University of Rochester. Department of Rare Books, Manuscripts, and Archives. Arthur T. Lee papers.

Washington, D.C. National Archives. Record Group 94, Microcopy 617, Roll 70. Fort Croghan Post Returns, 1849–1852.

Newspapers

Rochester (New York) *Union and Advertiser*. 1865, 1866, 1868, 1869, 1873, 1879.
Rochester (New York) *Democrat and Chronicle*. 1879.

Government Documents

"Echols Diary." In *Report of the Secretary of War*, 36th Cong., 2d sess., 1862. Senate Exec. Doc. No. 1.

Emory, William H. *Report on the United States and Mexican Boundary Survey*. 34th Cong., 1st sess., 1857. House Exec. Doc. No. 135. 2 vols.

The War of the Rebellion: Compilation of the Official Records of the Union and Confederate Armies. 130 vols. Washington, D.C.: War Department, 1880–1901.

Books and Articles

Bartlett, John R. *Personal Narrative of Explorations and Incidents in Texas, New Mexico, California, Sonora and Chihuahua*. 2 vols. New York, 1854.

Dodge, Richard Irving. *Our Wild Indians: Thirty-three Years' Personal Experience among the Red Men of the Great West*. Hartford, Conn.: A. D. Worthington, 1882.

Lane, Lydia Spencer. *I Married a Soldier*. Albuquerque, N.M.: Wallace Publications, 1964.

Lee, Arthur T. *Army Ballads and Other Poems*. N.p., 1871.

———. "Reminiscences of the Regiment," in *History of the Eighth U.S. Infantry*. Ed. Thomas Wilhelm. New York, 1871.

Mansfield, J. K. F. "Colonel J. K. F. Mansfield's Report on the Inspection of the Department of Texas in 1856," ed. M. L. Crimmins, *Southwestern Historical Quarterly* 42 (April, 1939): 351–357.

Spofford, Harriet Prescott. "San Antonio de Bexar," *Harper's Magazine* 55 (November, 1877): 831–850.

Stacey, May Humphreys. *Uncle Sam's Camels: The Journal of May Humphreys Stacey, Supplemented by the Report of Edward Fitzgerald Beale*. Ed. Lewis Burt Lesley. Cambridge, Mass.: Harvard University Press, 1929.

Trowbridge, Francis Bacon. *The Ashley Genealogy*. New Haven, Conn., 1896.

Whiting, William H. C. "Journal of William Henry Chase Whiting, 1849." In *Exploring Southwestern Trails, 1846–1854*. Ed. Ralph P. Bieber. Glendale, Calif.: Arthur H. Clark Co., 1938.

Wilhelm, Thomas. *Synopsis of the History of the Eighth U.S. Infantry and the Military Record of Officers*. David's Island, N.Y., 1871.

SECONDARY SOURCES

Books

Bender, Averam B. *The March of Empire: Frontier Defense in the Southwest, 1848–1860*. Lawrence: The University Press of Kansas, 1952.

Conkling, Roscoe Platt, and Conkling, Margaret Badenoch. *The Butterfield Overland Mail, 1857–1869*. 3 vols. Glendale, Calif.: Arthur H. Clark Co., 1947.

Corning, Leavitt, Jr. *Baronial Forts of the Big Bend*. San Antonio: Trinity University Press, 1967.

Day, James M. "Fort Davis." In *Frontier Forts of Texas*. Waco, Texas: Texian Press, 1966.

Frazer, Robert Walter. *Forts of the West*. Norman: University of Oklahoma Press, 1965.

Goetzmann, William H. *Army Exploration in the American West, 1803–1863*. New Haven, Conn.: Yale University Press, 1959.

Green, Rena Maverick, ed. *Samuel Maverick, Texan: 1803–1870*. San Antonio, 1952.

Greer, James K. *Colonel Jack Hays, Texas Frontier Leader and California Land Builder*. New York, 1952.

Haley, J. Evetts. *Fort Concho and the Texas Frontier*. San Angelo, Texas: San Angelo *Standard-Times*, 1952.

Hine, Robert V. *Bartlett's West: Drawing the Mexican Boundary*. New Haven, Conn.: Yale University Press, 1968.

Hodge, Frederick W., ed. *Handbook of American Indians North of Mexico*. 2 vols. Washington, D.C.: Bureau of American Ethnology, 1907.

Jackson, W. Turrentine. *Wagon Roads West: A Study of Federal Road Surveys and Construction in the Trans-Mississippi West, 1846–1869*. Berkeley: University of California Press, 1952.

Leckie, William H. *The Buffalo Soldiers: A Narrative of the Negro Cavalry in the West*. Norman: University of Oklahoma Press, 1967.

Pinckney, Pauline A. *Painting in Texas: The Nineteenth Century*. Austin: University of Texas Press, 1965.

Raht, Carlysle Graham. *The Romance of Davis Mountains and Big Bend Country*. Odessa, Texas: Rahtbooks, 1963.

Scobee, Barry, *Fort Davis, Texas, 1853–1960*. Fort Davis, Texas, 1963.

———. *Old Fort Davis*. San Antonio: The Naylor Co., 1947.

Tyler, Ronnie C. *The Big Bend: A History of the Last Texas Frontier*. Washington, D.C.: Department of the Interior, National Park Service, 1975.

Utley, Robert M. *Fort Davis National Historic Site, Texas*. Washington, D.C.: Department of the Interior, National Park Service, 1965.

Webb, Walter Prescott. *The Texas Rangers*. Rev. ed. Austin: University of Texas Press, 1965.

———, ed. *The Handbook of Texas*. Austin: Texas State Historical Association, 1952.

Wheat, Carl I. *Mapping the Transmississippi West, 1540–1861*. 5 vols. San Francisco, 1957–1963.

Wood, Leonard. *Our Military History: Its Facts and Fallacies*. Chicago: Reilly and Britton, 1916.

Articles

Bender, A. B. "Opening Routes across West Texas, 1848–1850," *Southwestern Historical Quarterly* 37 (October, 1933).

Cranmer, Neil D. "Chemung County's Part in the Civil War," *Chemung Historical Journal* 1 (September, 1955): 3–9.

Kurtz, Henry I. "A Soldier's Life," *American History Illustrated* 5 (August, 1972): 25–35.

Lammons, Bishop F. "Operation Camel: An Experiment in Animal Transportation in Texas, 1857–1860," *Southwestern Historical Quarterly* 61 (July, 1957).

Index